JOHN W. SCHAUM presents the
Best of Tchaikowsky
For PIANO SOLO

Foreword

The primary object of this album is to serve as an *introduction* to the music of Tchaikowsky. These arrangements enable a student of modest proficiency to gain an acquaintance with many master themes. Familiar music has been selected for maximum student appeal.

The choice of music in the collection is determined by its effectiveness for *teaching* purposes — based on thirty five years'

experience with thousands of piano students at the Schaum Music School in Wisconsin.

Additional books in this series are:
Best of BACH
Best of BEETHOVEN
Best of BRAHMS
Best of CHOPIN
Best of LISZT
Best of MOZART
Best of RACHMANINOFF
Best of SCHUBERT

EXCLUSIVELY DISTRIBUTED BY

HAL•LEONARD®
CORPORATION
7777 W. BLUEMOUND RD. P.O. BOX 13819 MILWAUKEE, WI 53213

Biographical Sketch

Peter Ilyitch Tchaikowsky (chy-CUFF-skee), the renowned master composer, was born in Russia on May 7, 1840. Piano lessons were begun at the age of seven. He made good, but by no means phenomenal progress. However, he always had a passionate love for music. His parents ignored this aptitude and encouraged law as a profession. Dutifully, he graduated from law school in 1859. In time, his musical talent manifested itself more and more and his interest in law declined. In 1861, he resigned his government post in the Ministry of Justice and began to devote himself exclusively to music. He studied theory, harmony and composition very intensively and in 1865 graduated with honors from the Conservatory in the city of Petrograd (now called Leningrad). In 1866, he became professor of harmony at the Moscow Conservatory. From this point on, his musical career flourished.

He had an extravagant need for fashionable clothes and luxurious living. Frequently, he spent more than his budget allowed. Consequently, he was often in economic difficulties. By a unique stroke of fate, he acquired the financial support of a wealthy patroness, Mme. von Meck. Her money supported him for thirteen years. During these years, Tchaikowsky produced some of his grandest works. Curiously, the composer and his benefactress never met.

His personal life was one of unhappiness. Serious emotional problems prevented him from making a successful marital adjustment. Deprived of this, music became his magnificent obsession. Here he poured out

◆ TCHAIKOWSKY ◆
1840 - 1893

his soul in creating some of the world's most exotic music. He has oftentimes used native folk material in his works. He was a zealous exponent of national spirit and color in music. His music shows strange and violent contrasts of mood: now full of fiery intensity; now of tenderness; now of melancholy.

Tchaikowsky was in demand as an orchestral conductor. In May, 1891, he visited America, conducting four concerts in New York as part of the dedication ceremony of Carnegie Hall. He died of cholera in his homeland, November 6, 1893.

Contents

The complete **NUTCRACKER SUITE** (along with four added numbers from the original ballet) is available in a separate album, arranged by John W. Schaum.

Romance

P. I. Tchaikowsky, Op. 5
Arr. by John W. Schaum

None but the Lonely Heart

P. I. Tchaikowsky
Arr. by John W. Schaum

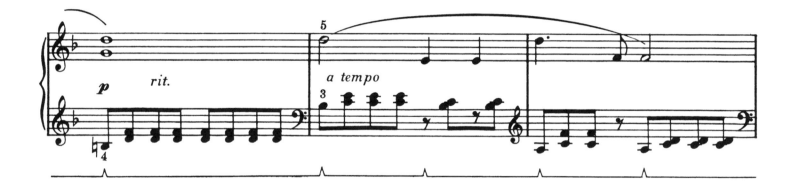

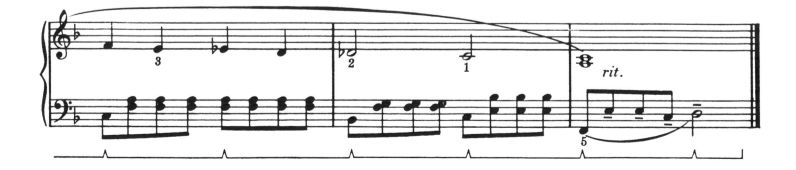

Italian Caprice

P. I. Tchaikowsky
Arr. by John W. Schaum

Allegretto

6

Waltz from Swan Lake

P. I. Tchaikowsky
Arr. by John W. Schaum

Tempo di Valse

Swan Lake Finale

P. I. Tchaikowsky, Op.20
Arr. by John W. Schaum

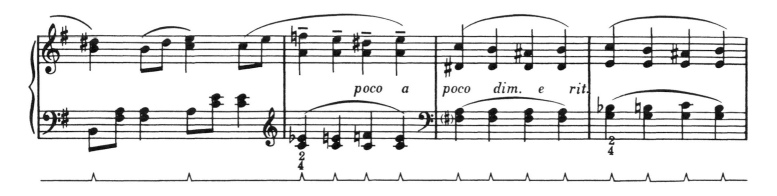

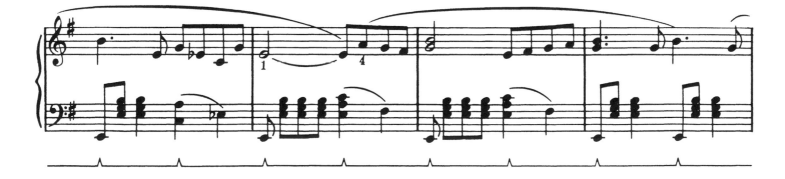

Song Without Words

P. I. Tchaikowsky, Op. 2, No. 3
Arr. by John W. Schaum

Allegretto

Sleeping Beauty Waltz

P. I. Tchaikowsky
Arr. by John W. Schaum

Tranquillo

March Slav

P. I. Tchaikowsky, Op. 31
Arr. by John W. Schaum

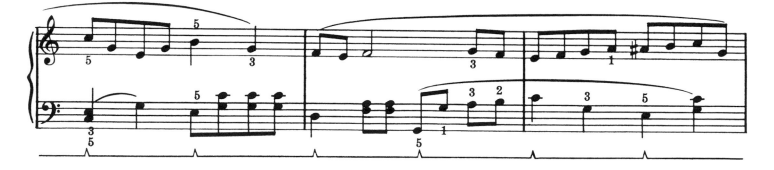

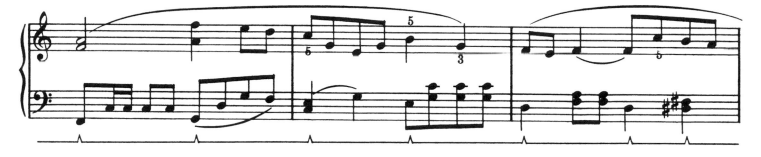

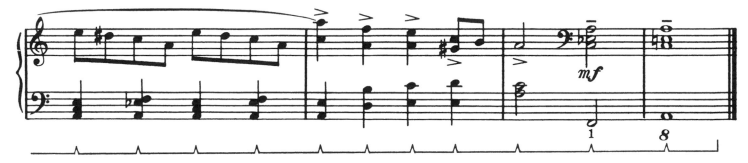

Serenade for Strings

P. I. Tchaikowsky Op. 48
Arr. by John W. Schaum

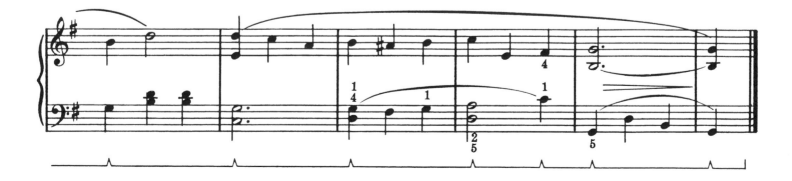

Chanson Triste

P. I. Tchaikowsky, Op.40, No.2
Arr. by John W. Schaum

Sweet Dreams

P. I. Tchaikowsky
Arr. by John W. Schaum

Andante

Eugene Onegin Waltz

P. I. Tchaikowsky
Arr. by John W. Schaum

Giocoso

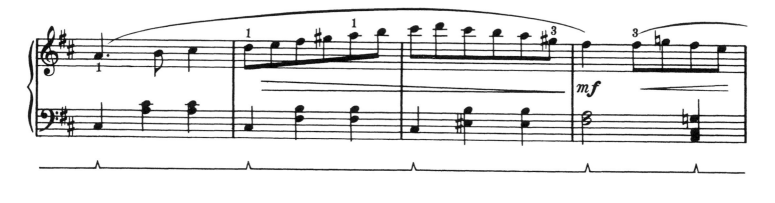

Romeo and Juliet Love Theme

P. I. Tchaikowsky
Arr. by John W. Schaum

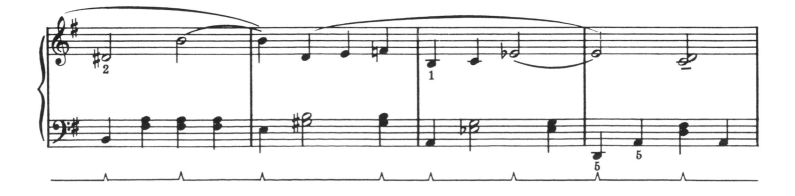

Piano Concerto Theme

P. I. Tchaikowsky
Arr. by John W. Schaum

Maestoso

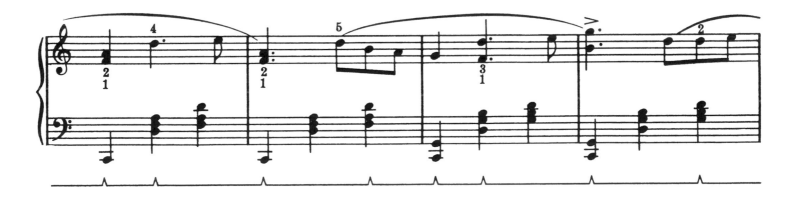

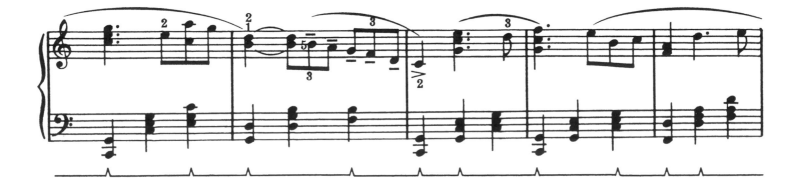

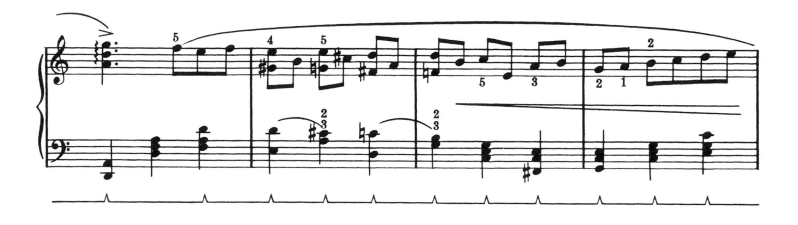

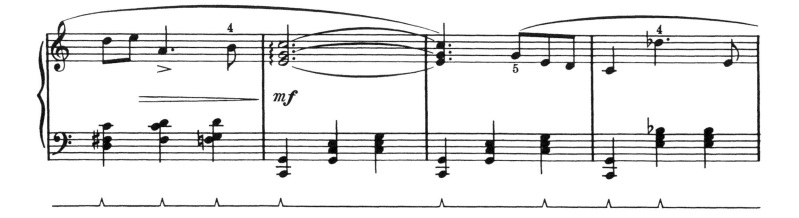

THEMES by the MASTERS ... Every Student Should Know

All Titles — LEVEL FOUR

- ♦ Music Selected for its EFFECTIVENESS in TEACHING

- ♦ Each Book Includes BIOGRAPHICAL DATA and COMPOSER PORTRAIT

- ♦ Collections Include Themes from SYMPHONIES, CHAMBER MUSIC, VOCAL LITERATURE, OPERA and PIANO

BEST OF BACH
INCLUDES: Air for G String — Bouree
Gavotte — Jesu, Joy of Man's Desiring
March in D Major — Minuet in G Major
Minuet in G Minor — Musette
My Heart Ever Faithful — Siciliano

BEST OF BEETHOVEN
INCLUDES: Andante from 5th Symphony
Bagatelle — Ecossaise — Fur Elise
Heavens Declare His Glory
Minuet from Sonata Op.49, No.2
Minuet in G — Moonlight Sonata

BEST OF MOZART
INCLUDES: Air in C (Marriage of Figaro)
Allegro in B-flat, K3 — Lullaby
Hand in Hand (Don Giovanni)
Minuet (Symphony in E-flat)
Overture (Marriage of Figaro)

Excerpt from "BEST OF BEETHOVEN"

BEST OF SCHUBERT

CONTENTS:
Cradle Song
Hark, Hark, the Lark
Impromptu, Op.142, No.2
Love Theme (from "Unfinished Symphony")
March Militaire
Minuet from Sonata, Op.78
Moment Musical, Op.94, No.3
Rosamunde Ballet Music, Op.26
Serenade
Sweet Repose (Du bist die Ruh')
Theme from Octet, Op.166
Trout
Valses Nobles, Op.77
Waltz in C

BEST OF TCHAIKOWSKY

CONTENTS:
Chanson Triste
Eugene Onegin Waltz
Italian Caprice
March Slav
None But the Lonely Heart
Piano Concerto Theme
Romance
Romeo and Juliet Love Theme
Serenade for Strings
Sleeping Beauty Waltz
Song Without Words
Swan Lake Finale
Sweet Dreams
Waltz from Swan Lake